table of Contents

clever cover-ups

Slipcovers

- 2 give 'em the slip
- 6 a better bistro
- 8 letter perfect
- 10 pinstriped pinafore
- 12 barstool beauty
- 14 so-soft checkerboard
- 17 dressmaker details
- 22 easy-living slipcovers
- 26 dressing table skirt
- 28 totally tailored ottoman
- 30 all buckled up
- 32 feel-good felt
- 34 slipcover basics

Upholstery

- 36 tailored headboard
- 39 printed perfection
- 41 pretty in piping
- 44 the look of leather
- 46 upholstery basics

From the Staff

What makes life so interesting is that things evolve. Seasons, trends, our own personal tastes —it seems our lives revolve around change. So when we turn to our homes, it's natural that we feel compelled to rearrange the furniture, remodel what we've outgrown, and redo just for the fun of it. This book helps you feel at home by offering slipcover and upholstery options that blend with your current style. You'll find that transforming your furniture is a fulfilling and cost-efficient way to get the look you want in your decor. So go ahead, follow our lead and make some creative cover-ups. Because, after all, change is good.

Enjoy!

Clever Cover-ups 1

Old chairs? Who would know? These dressy slipcovers add charm and personality no matter what the look underneath.

give 'em the Slip

what you'll need

decorator fabric
muslin (see "Making a Muslin Pattern," *page 34*)
thread (either matching or contrasting, depending on the desired look)
extra fabric for ruffles, pleats, or tabs (see "Embellishing Your Slipcover," *page 34*)
baubles, such as ribbon or silk flowers
fabric measuring tape
sewing machine with needle suited to the decorator fabric
fabric-marking pencil or pen
straightedge
fabric scissors, or rotary cutter and cutting mat
straight pins
T-pins
masking tape
graph paper and pencil
iron and ironing board

here's how

1 Visualize the chair as a combination of parts—for example, a front, back, seat, and skirt. Label each part with masking tape and a pen to prevent confusion later.

2 Use a fabric measuring tape to find the length and width of each part, noting where each begins and ends. Include the thickness of the chair back in either the front or back measurement, and decide where the arm seams should fall.

3 Double-check all measurements; then write down each part's dimensions. Add ½ inch to each edge for seam allowances; add 2 inches more for a hem at the bottom, and adjust for any pleats (see "Embellishing Your Slipcover," *page 34*). To determine how much fabric you'll need, make a cutting diagram: Draw your desired fabric (most are 54 inches wide) to scale on graph paper, then sketch the pieces you'll need on top. If you choose large-scale patterned fabric, purchase extra for matching. Use masking tape to mark a line down the center of each chair part to use later when assembling the muslin pattern.

4 To make the pattern and finish the slipcover, see *pages 34–35*.

a better Bistro

Bistro chairs, excelling in style and convenience, often lack in comfort. Soften both the look and feel of wood or metal chairs with brightly patterned padded covers.

what you'll need

fabric scissors
polyester quilt batting
fabric for the cover
fabric glue
4¼ yards cording or ribbon for ties
hook-and-loop tape
sewing machine with needle suited for fabric
thread

here's how

1 Cut batting to fit around the top of the chair back to cover the front, back, and upper edge. Cut fabric twice the length and twice the width of the batting. Center the batting on the wrong side of the fabric. Tack it in place with small dots of fabric glue. Fold the top and bottom edges of the fabric to the center of the batting and glue or slip-stitch in place. Fold the remaining two edges in toward the center and glue or slip-stitch them in place.

2 Fold the chair-back cover over the chair top. Tack 16-inch-long ties to each corner and tie the cover in place.

3 Cut two strips of batting for the seat, one to go lengthwise and one to go crosswise. Let the batting drape 6 to 8 inches over the edge on all sides. Cover each batting strip in the same manner as the chair back.

4 Place one panel to drape over the sides on the seat. Place the top cover over it, centering both pieces. Glue the soft loop side of hook-and-loop tape to the underside of the top panel along the outer edges. Glue the rigid loop side of the hook-and-loop tape to the side panel in the corresponding spots.

5 Tack 16-inch-long ties to the back corners and tie the seat cover to the chair.

letter Perfect

Plain fabric accented with an appliquéd monogram and piping creates a formal look. Use one letter for all the chairs or give each chair its own initial.

what you'll need

- fabric measuring tape
- 54-inch-wide fabric (about 3 yards, but the amount will vary with chair size)
- fabric scissors
- kraft paper for pattern
- contrasting nonwoven (nonfraying) fabric for the monogram, such as imitation suede
- paper-backed fusible webbing
- computer-generated letter for monogram or stencil (the one shown measures 10×7 inches)
- 2 yards of ¼-inch-diameter piping or cording
- pins
- thread
- sewing machine with needle suited to the fabric

here's how

1 Measure the chair seat width and depth. For the skirt width, double the seat depth and add the seat front width, plus 36 inches for box pleats, back closure, and hems. For the skirt length, measure the seat height, and add 2½ inches for the seam allowances and hem. Cut out the skirt piece.

2 Trace the seat shape onto paper. Add ½-inch seam allowances around the side and front edges. Extend the seat shape 20 inches in the back to create a flap that will hang to the floor with a 2-inch-wide hem. Add ½-inch seam allowances to make the sides and length of the flap. Make small notches in this piece to fit around the structure of the chair. Cut out the paper pattern and try it on the chair. Make adjustments if needed; then cut out the seat from the fabric.

3 Fuse the paper-backed fusible webbing to the contrasting monogram fabric. Trace the letter onto fabric and cut out. Peel off the backing and center the letter on the seat. Fuse it in place according to the manufacturer's directions. If you wish, sew around the appliqué with a narrow, tight zigzag (satin stitch) to hold it in place.

4 Using handmade or purchased piping, sew the piping to the seat along the seam line. Sew the piping to the front and sides only. Cut enough 2-inch-wide bias strips to cover the needed amount of piping cord to fit the seat plus 6 inches for overlap. See Steps 16–18 on *pages 24–25* for piping assembly instructions.

5 Hem one long bottom edge and both short edges of the skirt. Pin the center of the skirt to the center front of the seat with right sides facing and raw edges aligned. Pin out toward the corners. At each corner, fold back 3 inches of skirt fabric, then fold the fabric forward again. Repeat in the opposite direction to make box pleats. Continue pinning the skirt around the seat. Sew the skirt to the seat. Clip the fabric seams.

6 Cut four 12×1-inch ties. Hem the short edges. Turn the long edges under ¼ inch; then fold the ties in half lengthwise encasing the raw edges. Topstitch along both edges. Tack one end of one tie to the top of the skirt back and a second tie to the center of the skirt back. Repeat for the other end of the skirt back.

7 Place the slipcover over the chair and tie the ties. Flip the back flap over the back of the skirt.

pinstriped Pinafore

A scallop-edge pinstripe cover looks like a pretty little pinafore. The curves of the bottom are a good match for the shapely rounded top.

what you'll need

fabric measuring tape
medium-weight fabric (the amount will vary with the chair height and size)
fabric scissors
water-erasable fabric marker
kraft paper for pattern
straight pins
sewing machine with needle suited to the fabric
thread

here's how

1 For the length of the main panel, start at the rear of the chair and measure from the seat, over the back, down to the seat, and across the seat to the front edge. Add 10 inches to each end. For the width, use the seat width and add 1-inch seam allowances.

2 For the side panels, cut two pieces of fabric 10 inches long plus the depth of the chair seat; add 1-inch seam allowances. Cut one main panel and two side panels. Hem the short ends of the side panels.

3 Make a paper pattern for the front and sides, dividing the panel measurements into three scallops. Turn up a 5-inch-wide hem on each end of the main panel, right sides facing. Transfer the curved line to the bottom of the hem. Sew along the line. Clip curves and trim seam allowances. Repeat for the back. Turn the hem to the back side; press. Make the hemline for the side panels in the same manner.

4 Place the main panel over the chair and pin in place. Lay one side panel across the seat, right side down. Align one long edge with the side of the seat cover; pin in place. Repeat for the other side panel. Sew the panels to the main panel.

5 To form the upper curve of the main panel, place the cover on the chair, wrong side out. Carefully mark the curve of the upper edge of the chair. Sew ½ inch outside the line through both layers of fabric. Turn the cover to the right side and try it on the chair. If the fit is correct, trim away the excess fabric.

6 Hem the long edges of the slipcover, encasing the raw edges. Place the cover over the chair and mark the placement for the ribbon ties. Tack the ribbons in place and tie the slipcover to the chair.

Add extra comfort to wood barstools with tie-on pillows and flouncy skirted slipcovers.

barstool Beauty

what you'll need

fabric measuring tape
blue floral fabric for slipcover, flange, and ties
  lining fabric
blue-and-cream ticking for covered piping
yellow-blue-and-cream plaid for skirt
fabric scissors
¼-inch-diameter cotton piping cord
2½-inch-diameter covered button
polyester fiberfill
sewing machine with needle suited to fabric
thread

here's how

Note: Quantities specified are for 52/54-inch-wide decorator fabrics. All measurements include ½-inch seam allowances unless otherwise noted. Sew with right sides together unless otherwise stated.

For the slipcover, trace the chair seat shape onto tracing paper, adding ½ inch seam allowances all around before purchasing fabrics. Fabric yardages will depend on the size of the chair seat.

For the pillow, you may wish to modify the size to fit the width of the back of your chair. When determining the cut length for the pillow ties, consider cutting two of the tie strips longer than the other two (the length will depend on the size of your chair back). Pair one long and one short tie together so they are even when tied into a bow.

1 Prepare to cut the fabrics for the slipcover.
From the floral fabric, cut:
1 slipcover top (use traced chair seat
  for pattern)
4–3-inch-wide strips for ties (cut to desired
  length to fit your chair)
From the lining fabric, cut:
1 slipcover top lining (use traced chair seat
  for pattern)

2 Determine the size to cut the flange and skirt pieces. Measure the distance along one side of the barstool, around the front, and along the opposite side. Cut one 3-inch-wide flange piece from floral fabric at the determined length plus the seam allowance at the ends. Cut one 6½-inch-wide skirt piece at two times the determined length.

3 To assemble the slipcover, sew a ¼-inch hem along one long edge of the skirt piece; press. Gather the skirt piece along the remaining long raw edge to correspond with the cut width of the flange piece; pin to the matching flange piece. Sew the skirt piece to the flange piece. Sew a narrow hem along the side edge of the flange/skirt piece.

4 Fold each tie strip in half lengthwise with right sides together and raw edges aligned. Sew along the long side and one short side of each strip, leaving one short side open; trim the corners. Turn strips right side out through the opening; press. Baste the ties to the back edge of the cushion top, positioning as necessary to fit chair.

5 With right sides facing, sew the cushion top to the lining along the back edge, leaving an opening. Turn cushion to right side; press. Baste side and front raw edges together.

6 Cut 1½-inch-wide bias strips from the ticking fabric to make enough covered piping to cover two side edges and the front edge of the slipcover. Sew the strips around the cord to make one continuous length as shown. Sew the cord to the sides and the front of the slipcover top.

7 With right sides facing, sew the flange/skirt piece around the sides and front of the slipcover top.

8 Prepare to cut the fabrics for the pillow.
From the floral fabric, cut:
2–8½×14-inch rectangles
4–3-inch-wide strips for ties (cut to desired
  lengths to fit around chair back)

9 Cut enough 1½-inch-wide strips to make 1⅓ yards. Cover the piping cord and sew the strips around the cord to make one continuous length. Beginning at the center of one long edge, pin the covered piping cord to the right side of one panel, aligning the raw edges. Where the piping meets, overlap the ends 1 inch and cut the excess. Remove the stitching in each end of the fabric cover. Unfold the fabric and cut the ends of the cord to meet. Refold one cover end under the cord. On the remaining end, turn the cover under ½ inch and refold the fabric around the cord, concealing the raw edges of the fabric cover. Using a zipper foot and a long stitch length, baste the covered piping to the front panel; clip and pivot the stitching at the corners.

10 Referring to step 4, make the ties. Baste the ties in sets of two to the front panel, positioning them as necessary to fit the chair.

11 Sew the front panel to the back panel. Using a zipper foot and a normal stitch length, stitch the back to the front along the basting line; pivot the stitching at the corners. Leave a long opening along one side; trim the corners. Press the seam.

12 Turn the cover right side out, pushing out the corners. Press the seam. Firmly stuff the pillow with fiberfill. Sew the opening closed.

13 Use floral fabric to cover the button according to the manufacturer's instructions. Sew it to the center front of the pillow, pulling the thread tightly to tuft it slightly.

Little hands can help weave the fleece strips and tie the skirt onto the chair seat. With hundreds of colors of fleece available at fabric stores, you can select fleece colors to coordinate with almost any room decor.

so-soft Checkerboard

what you'll need

fabric measuring tape
fabric scissors
straight pins
fabric glue
washable fabric-marking pen
¾ yard apple green fleece
1 yard yellow fleece
1 yard chartreuse fleece
¼ yard mint green fleece
¼ yard teal fleece
blanket batting
sewing machine with needle suited to the fabric
matching sewing thread

here's how

CHAIR SKIRT

1 Measure the chair seat with a fabric tape measure. Add 1 inch to the width and depth measurements to allow for seam allowances. Using these measurements, cut out the cushion top and bottom from apple green fleece. You may need to cut notches in the back of the cushion pieces to fit around the chair back. Cut out blanket batting using the chair-seat measurements without the added seam-allowance measurement. With wrong sides together, layer the cushion top and bottom with the batting in the middle. Sew around all edges.

2 From yellow fleece, cut a front underskirt 10 inches long and the width of the front and two sides of the chair seat. Cut a back underskirt 10 inches long and the width of the back of the chair seat. Cut four overskirt pieces from chartreuse fleece. Each overskirt should be 8 inches long and the width of the corresponding side of the chair seat. Cut 2-inch-wide scallops along the bottom edges of the overskirt and underskirt pieces. On the four overskirts, mark with washable fabric-marking pen 6-inch-long vertical slits, spaced 1 to 2 inches from each edge and 2 inches apart. Cut along the marked lines.

Cut larger pieces of fleece *parallel* to the selvage edge. This direction has less stretch and provides more strength to the finished piece.

3 From apple green, mint green, and teal fleece, cut four 2-inch-wide strips from each color; lengths of strips should correspond to the widths of the overskirts. Weave strips through the overskirt slits, alternating the weave of each strip. Tack ends into place with fabric glue or sew with a basting stitch.

4 With right sides up, baste overskirts to the corresponding underskirts. With right sides together, pin the overskirt/underskirt sections to the cushion. Sew in place. Cut two ½×24-inch ties from apple green fleece. Sew the center portion of each tie to one back corner of the cushion, extending the sewing around the notches if applicable. Place the cushion on the seat and tie.

CHAIR TOPPER

1 From yellow fleece, cut an undertopper 26 inches long and 1 inch wider than the width of the chair back. From chartreuse fleece, cut an overtopper the same width as the undertopper and 22 inches long (the undertopper will extend 2 inches longer than the overtopper). Adjust the length in 2-inch increments to suit your chair if necessary.

2 Cut 2-inch-wide scallops along the short edges of the yellow and chartreuse toppers. Using a fabric-marking pen on the chartreuse overtopper, mark cutting lines parallel to the long edges, spaced 1 to 2 inches from the long edges, 2 inches from the scalloped edges, and 2 inches apart. Cut along the marked lines.

3 Cut nine 2-inch-wide strips the width of the chair topper plus 1 inch: two from teal fleece, three from apple green fleece, and four from mint green fleece. (Adjust the number of strips to suit your topper length.) Weave the strips through the slits, starting with apple green in center. Follow on either side with mint green, then teal, then remaining apple green and mint green strips, alternating the weave of each strip. Pin the strips in place.

4 With right sides up, center the overtopper on the undertopper. Fold the entire chair topper in half with right sides together so the scalloped edges meet. Match up the woven rows (colors should match) and pin in place. Sew side seams through all layers and turn the topper right side out. Slide the topper over the chair back.

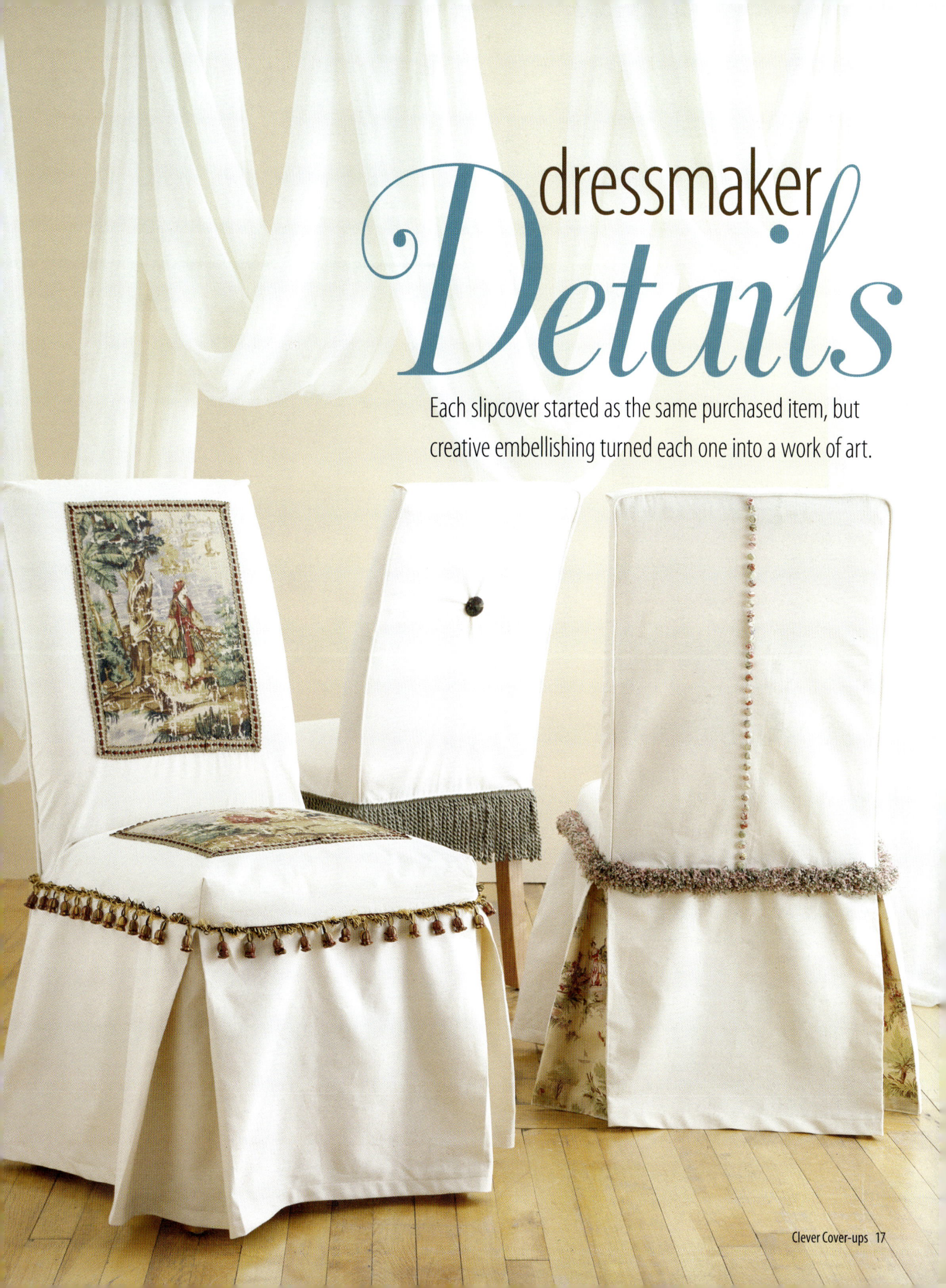

dressmaker
Details

Each slipcover started as the same purchased item, but creative embellishing turned each one into a work of art.

Beginning with the blank canvas of a plain purchased dining chair slipcover, it's the addition of decorative fabric panels, trims, and dressmaker details that gives each of these slipcovers its own *style.*

PRETTY AS A PICTURE
Panels cut from toile or another patterned fabric are an elegant and practical option for embellishing the seat and seat back of a slipcover, *below*. To reduce puckering and shifting of the panels as the chair is used, use fusible web to attach the panels before topstitching gimp around the edges. Tassel fringe dresses up the top of the skirt.

BUTTON UP
Whatever your color scheme, get inspired by today's fashions and add coordinating fabric to diminutive covered buttons sewn down the center back of the slipcover *above* and *opposite*. The buttons are purely decorative and are stitched without matching buttonholes. A band of bushy fringe makes a soft and pretty edge around the slipcover seat.

Elevate inverted pleats to decorative accents with the addition of patterned fabric panels. A quaint toile country scene peeks out between the folds of the pleats at each corner of the slipcover bottom.

DARE TO DANGLE
Long bullion fringe hangs over and conceals the short skirt on the slipcover *below*, revealing the legs underneath. A large covered button pulled to a gather adds a point of interest to the seat back.

PERSONALIZE IT
If large family gatherings are common at your dining table, a monogrammed slipcover back for family members is a fun way to identify seat assignments, *above*. Take advantage of your sewing machine's embroidery capabilities to stitch the monogram onto the back panel of a plain slipcover.

Purchase a plain slipcover and *embellish* it with trims and details, or make your own slipcover for a custom fit.

FANCY THAT
Pink-and-green cording outlines the edges of the seat and seat back on the chair *above*, and generous tassel fringe adds visual weight to the skirt edge. Coordinating covered buttons spaced at wide intervals along the back balance the use of trim.

CLASSIC COMBO
Wide black ribbon topstitched to the center of the slipcover back gets a touch of glamour with the addition of rhinestone costume jewelry pinned along the length. Playful pom-pom fringe bounces along the skirt edge.

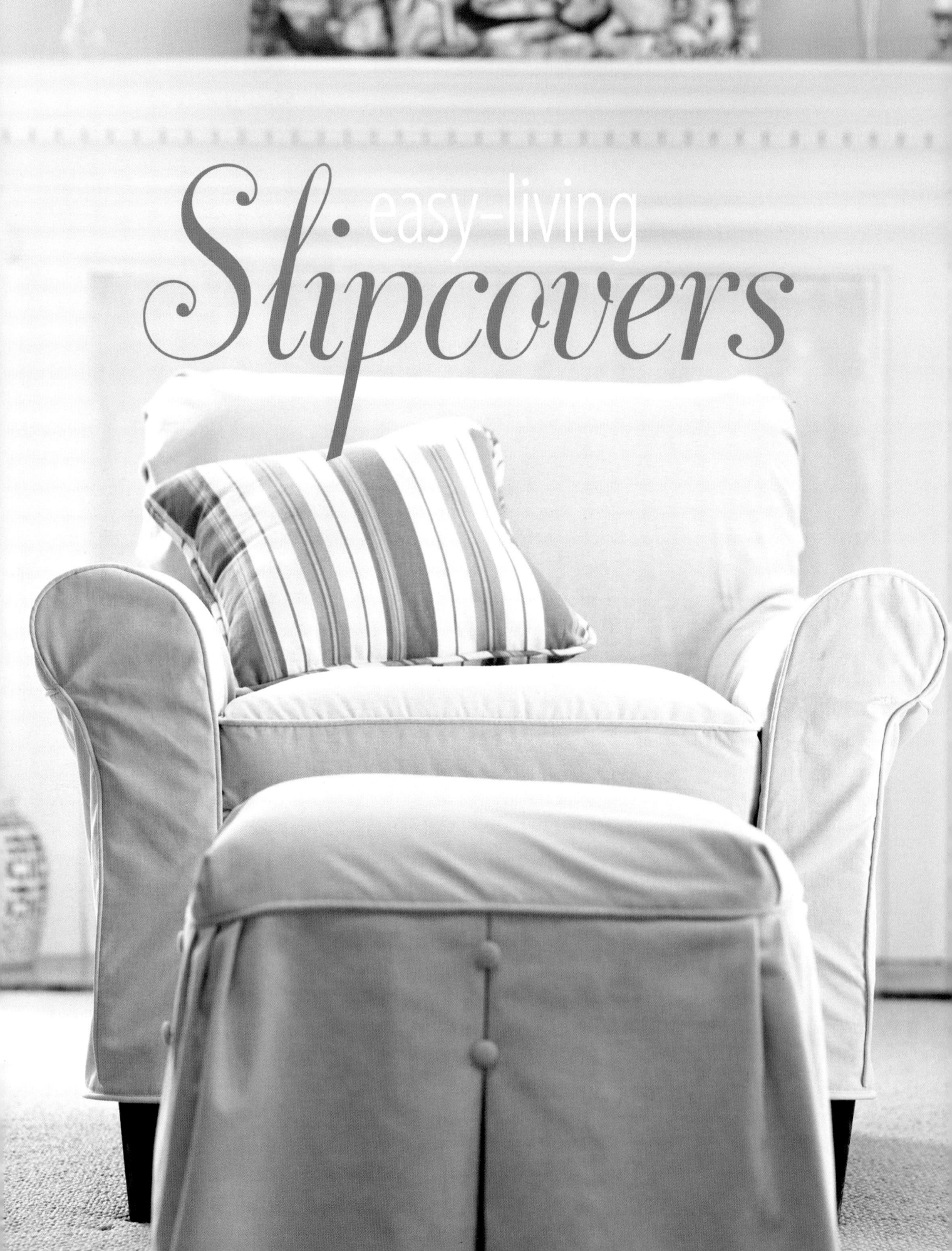

A slipcover redo does wonders for a once-mismatched armchair and ottoman. Stitched with inexpensive canvas and enhanced with details such as tucks, fabric-covered buttons, pleats, and piping, a slipcover set is one way to update your furniture without breaking the budget.

what you'll need

(for one chair and one ottoman)
fabric measuring tape
T-pins
fabric scissors
8–10 yards of fabric for chair
3 yards of fabric for ottoman
15–20 yards of 5/32-inch cording
18 inches of hook-and-loop tape
8—1½-inch covered buttons for ottoman
tailor's chalk
zipper for cushion cover (or hook-and-loop tape)
sewing machine with needle suited to the fabric
zipper foot or piping foot for sewing machine
thread

here's how

Note: Quantities specified are for 44/45-inch-wide fabrics; adjust yardage requirements for your furniture and fabric (allowing for pattern repeats). Prewash fabric if shrinkage is a possibility. Use ¾ inch for seam allowances unless otherwise noted. Sew with matching sewing threads and with right sides together unless otherwise stated. Label the patterns on the wrong side of the fabric with the chalk.

For best results, you may want to cut chair pieces slightly larger than noted. It's always easier to trim away a little excess fabric than to recut new, larger pieces. Pin the pieces to the chair with the right sides facing out. Except for the main Body piece, you will be creating fabric pieces for only one-half of the chair cover; the pinned half-cover will be removed, and then the remaining pieces will be cut. Label all patterns on the wrong side of the fabric with the chalk.

CHAIR

1 Remove the cushion; measure and mark the center of the chair by inserting pins into the chair every 12 inches so the pins run up the seat front, the deck (the seat bottom where the cushion sits), the inside back, and then down the outside back of the chair (like a center highway line). See the chair diagram on *page 24.*

2 Measure the width of the inside back from seam to seam at the widest point and add 2 inches for seam allowances. Measure the height of the inside back from the deck to the top of the inside back (to the existing chair seam) and add 2 inches. Cut a piece of fabric to these measurements.

3 Measure the depth of the deck and down the seat front and add 2 inches to this measurement. Cut a piece of fabric with these measurements (place the selvage edge running horizontally).

4 With right sides facing and using 1-inch seams, sew the two pieces together along one short edge to form the Body of the piece. Press the seam open.

5 Fold the Body in half lengthwise with right sides facing and raw edges even. Use chalk to mark the center fold on the wrong side of the fabric. Place the fabric right side out over the chair, working from the top of the inside back down to the deck and allowing 1 inch for a seam allowance at the top. Align the chalked line with the pins; then smooth (but do not pull too tightly) the fabric and pin it to the

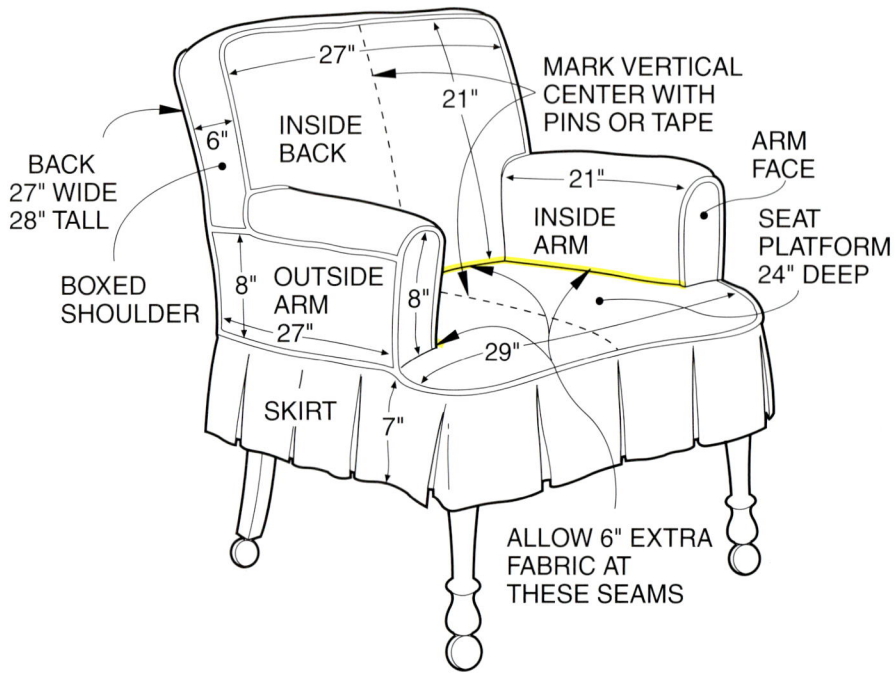

inside back, anchoring the shape. Continue smoothing and pinning the fabric to the deck and seat front. With tailor's chalk, mark the outline of the Body (do not scrimp); also lightly mark the hemline; trim the fabric 2 inches below the chalk line. **Note:** Trim only the hemline; the rest of the fabric will be trimmed later.

6 Measure the Outside Arm panel, adding 4 inches to the length and width measurements. Cut one Outside Arm panel to these measurements. Pin the panel to the chair, allowing for the seam allowance at the top. With chalk, lightly mark the hemline; trim the fabric 2 inches below the chalk line.

7 Take measurements for the Inside Arm panel; add 2 inches to each measurement for seams. Cut a panel to these measurements.

8 Measure and cut a piece for the Arm Front, adding 1 inch seam allowances to the top and sides and 3 inches to the bottom.

9 Remove the Outside Arm panel. With wrong sides facing, pin the Inside Arm panel to the Outside Arm panel along the top edge, placing pins along the seam allowance. Place the piece wrong side down over the arm of the chair.

10 Take the width and length measurements for the Back of the chair, adding 4 inches to both. Cut out the Back from fabric; pin the fabric Back to the back of the chair, starting in the center and working to the outer edge. Pin the Back and Body pieces together along the seam allowance (around the top curved half of the chair), making small tucks in the Body as needed to ease it in place. Do not pull the fabric too tightly; the slipcover should be a relaxed fit.

11 Continue pinning down the back of the chair along the seam allowance, pinning the Back to the Outside and Inside Arm panels. Pin the Inside Arm to the Body at the decking. Pin the Arm Front to the Inside Arm, the Outside Arm, and the Body. Recheck and mark all hemlines, trimming the fabric 2 inches below the chalk line where necessary. One-half of the chair is covered.

12 Remove the anchor pins but not the seam-allowance pins. Gently lift the half-slipcover off the chair. Use the chalk to mark the seam allowances; then trim the seam allowances to measure ¾ inch (do not cut the opposite half of the Body or the Back yet). Use a pencil to mark the point on the wrong side where the Inside Arm/Outside Arm seam meets the Back. This mark will serve as a notch. Mark another notch on the Inside Arm seam where it joins the Body.

13 Remove all pins from the slipcover. Fold the Body in half and cut its opposite half. Do the same for the Back. Cut a matching Inside Arm and Outside Arm. With right sides of fabric facing, cut a second Arm Front. (You will now have one complete Body, one complete Back, two Inside Arms, two Outside Arms, and two Arm Fronts.)

14 For piping, cut and piece enough 2-inch-wide bias strips to equal 15 to 20 yards. Cutting strips on the bias makes the fabric easier to wrap around the cording and around the corners of your finished slipcover. To find the bias (a line diagonal to the grain of the fabric), make sure the edges of your fabric are cut along the grain. Fold one of the corners diagonally across the fabric, and finger-press the fold. The pressed line is the bias line.

15 The cut width of the bias strips should equal the circumference of the cord plus 1 inch for seam allowances. Align a clear acrylic ruler along the pressed line at the width you want to cut your bias strips. Use a rotary cutter to cut the strips along the edge of the ruler.

16 With right sides together, lay the strips at right angles to each other. Pin and sew diagonally 3/16 inch from the edge. Open and press the seam flat. Trim away the corners that extend beyond the strip edge.

17 Lay the cord in the center on the wrong side of the bias strip. Fold and pin the fabric over the cord, aligning the raw edges. Using a zipper foot or piping foot on your sewing machine, sew close to the cord along the length of the strip. The stitching should tightly encase the cord. Do not trim the seam allowance—it will be used to attach the piping to the slipcover. Cut the required length of piping for your slipcover, adding 4 inches for each joined length if needed.

18 Lay the piping on the right side of the fabric, aligning the raw cut-edge of the piping with the raw cut-edge of the fabric. Position the piping so the rounded side faces the center of the project; pin in place. Using a zipper foot or piping foot, baste the piping in place. To overlap two piping ends, unravel each end of the cording and cut out about half of the cording strands. Twist the two ends together, and hand-stitch around the twisted joint to hold it together. Re-cover the cording, folding the raw edge of the top strip under. With right sides facing, lay the backing panel on top of the panel with the attached piping. Using the basted seam line as a guide, sew through all fabric layers. Finish the project as directed.

19 Sew the piping to the seam allowance between the Outside and Inside Arm pieces, around the top curve of the Back, and around the Arm Front pieces. Set aside the extra piping.

20 With right sides facing, pin and sew the Back to the Body and the Outside and Inside Arm pieces, stopping 18 inches from the end. Turn under 1 inch twice around the bottom of the slipcover and topstitch the hem. Attach hook-and-loop fastening tape to the opening.

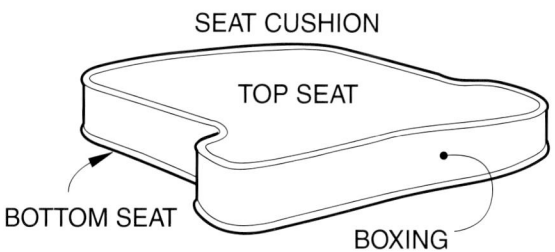

CHAIR CUSHION

1 Measure the depth and width of the seat cushion and add 1½ inches to each measurement for ¾-inch seam allowances. Cut two fabric pieces with these measurements for the seat cushion top and bottom. Sew piping around each piece.

2 Measure the height of the cushion and add 1½ inches. Measure the distance around the sides and front of the cushion; add 1½ inches. Cut a band of fabric to these measurements. Measure the width on the back of the cushion; add 3 inches to the height and 1½ inches to the width. Cut a band of fabric to these measurements. Fold the band in half lengthwise and cut along the fold. Insert a zipper (or hook-and-loop fastening tape) along the cut edges. With right sides facing, sew the short sides of the zippered band to the short sides of the front/sides band, forming a ring.

3 With right sides facing, pin and sew one edge of the band to one piped cushion piece. Mark the corners on the band. Open/unzip the cushion enough to create an opening for turning the cushion right side out. Pin and sew the opposite edge of the band to the remaining corded cushion piece. Turn the cover right side out, insert the seat cushion, and zip closed.

OTTOMAN

1 Measure the depth and width on the top of the ottoman; add 6 inches or more to both measurements (for a 3-inch drop) plus 3 inches to both measurements (twice the amount you'll need for ¾-inch seam allowances); cut one fabric piece with these measurements for the top. Pin the fabric to the top of the ottoman, pinning a tuck at each corner.

2 Measure from the top edge of the ottoman to the floor for the skirt; subtract the 3-inch drop from this measurement, then add 2 inches for the hem and ¾ inch for the top seam allowance. Measure around the ottoman where the skirt will meet the top; add 60 inches to this measurement (3 inches for tucks at each corner and 12 inches for each inverted center pleat). Cut and piece the fabric to these measurements.

3 Press a 1-inch-wide hem under twice along the bottom edge of the skirt; topstitch. Sew cording around the top. Place the cord-trimmed top on the ottoman; then pin the skirt to the top, forming three tucks around each corner and inverted pleats in the center of each side. Remove the skirt from the top, keeping the pins holding the tucks and pleats in place. Press the pleats. With right sides facing, pin; then sew the skirt to the top. Cover the buttons with fabric, following the manufacturer's directions. Hand-sew two buttons to each center pleat.

dressing table Skirt

Transform a vintage dressing table into an elegant place for touching up makeup. Gather metallic stripe fabric with shirring tape and adorn the bottom edge with brush fringe to make the flowing skirt.

what you'll need

fabric measuring tape
fabric scissors
metallic stripe polyester
lining fabric for table skirt lining
green, pink, and cream silk plaid for tabletop and topper skirt
fleece for tabletop lining
muslin for topper skirt lining
tracing paper; shirring tape
beaded-ball fringe and rust brush fringe
¼-inch-diameter cotton piping cord; thread
sewing machine with needle suited to the fabric

here how

Note: Quantities specified are for 52/54-inch-wide decorator fabrics. All measurements include ½-inch seam allowances unless otherwise noted. Sew with right sides together unless otherwise stated. Measure your own dressing table for accurate fabric yardages and cut sizes.

1 Measure the height of the dressing table. Measure the circumference of the tabletop.

2 Determine the size to cut the table skirt and table skirt lining. (Cut the lengths of the table skirt and the lining to equal the measured dressing table height plus a 2-inch-wide hem. Cut the widths of the table skirt and the lining to equal the measured circumference of the tabletop times 2 plus 1 inch for seam allowances.) For a large table, it may be necessary to seam together fabric widths to achieve the desired fullness. Cut one table skirt from metallic stripe polyester and one lining from the table skirt lining fabric. Join the pieces if necessary.

3 Use tracing paper to trace the shape of the tabletop, adding ¾ inch all around for seam allowances and ease; cut out the pattern. Use the pattern to cut one tabletop from silk plaid and one from fleece for the tabletop lining.

4 Determine the size to cut the topper skirt and the topper skirt lining. (Cut the length of the topper skirt to equal 7 inches. Cut the width of the topper skirt to equal the measured circumference of the tabletop plus 1-inch seam allowances plus ease.) Cut one topper skirt from silk plaid and one from muslin for the topper skirt lining.

5 To assemble the table skirt, press under and sew a 2-inch-wide hem along one long edge of the table skirt and table skirt lining. Press under and sew a ½-inch-wide hem along each side edge of the table skirt and table skirt lining. Layer the table skirt and table skirt lining together with wrong sides facing; pin together along the unhemmed edges. Pin shirring tape to the wrong side of the skirt along the unhemmed edge; sew through all layers, being careful not to stitch into the cords. Knot the cords together at one end. Pull the cords from the other end to evenly gather the fabric to the appropriate width. Tie the cord ends together.

6 Topstitch brush fringe to the bottom edge of the skirt.

7 To assemble the topper, baste the fleece tabletop lining to the wrong side of the tabletop piece.

8 Referring to the instructions in steps 14–18 on *pages 24–25* for making covered piping, cut enough 1¾-inch-wide bias strips from silk plaid to equal the circumference of the tabletop plus seam allowance. Sew the covered piping to the edges of the lined tabletop.

9 With right sides facing and matching one long edge, sew the muslin topper skirt lining to the topper skirt, overlapping the ends. Fold the muslin topper skirt lining up toward the back of the topper skirt and press in place. Matching long raw edges, sew the topper skirt to the lined tabletop.

10 Using coordinating thread, hand-sew beaded-ball fringe to the back bottom edge of the topper skirt.

11 Attach the skirt to the table using thumbtacks; then place the topper over the top of the table (the thumbtacks will be concealed underneath the topper).

totally tailored
Ottoman

A tailored slipcover edged in striped fabric brings clean lines to a large living room ottoman.

what you'll need

fabric measuring tape
fabric scissors
muslin
straight pins
washable fabric-marking pen
decorator fabric
sewing machine with needle suited to the fabric
thread

here's how

1 Measure the width and length of each surface you wish to cover, add 2 to 3 inches to each measurement, and then use fabric scissors to cut the top and side pattern pieces out of muslin. Center the muslin top piece on the ottoman top, and smooth to the edges. Pin the side pieces to the top piece and to each other. When you're pleased with the fit, mark the pinned lines on each muslin piece with a fabric-marking pen for sewing lines. Remove the pins and lay the muslin flat.

2 Draw a second line ½ inch outside each marked line for a seam allowance. Cut each muslin pattern piece along the outer lines. Pin the muslin pattern pieces onto the decorator fabric. Cut around the pattern and remove the muslin. With right sides facing and using ½-inch seam allowances, sew the side pieces to each other and then to the top piece.

3 To cover a round ottoman, make two muslin pattern pieces. For the skirt piece, determine the desired length and measure the circumference of the ottoman; add 2 inches on all sides. For the top piece, flip the ottoman upside down on the muslin and trace the shape with a fabric-marking pen; cut 2 inches outside the traced line. Fit the pattern pieces on the ottoman, pinning the skirt piece to the top piece and marking the sewing lines as for the rectangular ottoman. Use the pattern pieces to cut the decorator fabric to the correct size. Sew the skirt to the top piece; then sew the raw side edges of the skirt piece together.

4 For a border on either a rectangular or a round ottoman, cut enough 4-inch-wide bias strips from decorator fabric to total the perimeter of the skirt bottom plus seam allowances. With right sides facing and using ½-inch seam allowances, sew the strips together to make a large circle; press the seams open. Using a clothes iron, press under ½ inch on one long edge of the border strip. Position the border right side down on the wrong side of the skirt, aligning the unpressed edge with the bottom edge of the skirt; sew ½ inch from the edge. Fold the border over to the front of the skirt, and press. Sew the border in place along the inner pressed edge. Slip the finished cover over the ottoman.

Clever Cover-ups 29

all Buckled Up

In place of a coffee table, a plain ottoman slipcovered in menswear plaid offers a casual spot for a collection of accessories, such as an assortment of books and a teatime tray. A leather belt cinched around the perimeter is not only attractive but also practical as it holds the corner pleats snugly to the side of the ottoman.

what you'll need

fabric measuring tape
fabric scissors
2½–3 yards of fabric
2–3 yards of 5/32-inch cording
T-pins
tailor's chalk
belt(s) to wrap around ottoman
sewing machine with needle suited for fabric
thread

here's how

Note: Quantities specified are for 52/54-inch-wide fabrics; adjust yardage requirements for your furniture and fabric (allowing for fabric repeats). Prewash the fabric if shrinkage is a possibility. Use ¾ inch for seam allowances unless otherwise noted. Sew with matching sewing threads and with right sides together unless otherwise stated. Label the patterns on the wrong side of the fabric using the chalk.

1 Measure the depth and width on the top of the ottoman; add 3 inches to both measurements (twice the amount you'll need for ¾-inch seam allowances); cut one fabric piece with these measurements for the top. Pin the fabric to the top of the ottoman.

2 Measure from the top edge of the ottoman to the floor for the skirt; add 2 inches for the hem and ¾ inch for the top seam allowance. Measure around the ottoman at the point where the skirt will meet the top; add 48 inches to this measurement (12 inches for each inverted corner pleat). Cut and piece the fabric to these measurements.

3 Press under a 1-inch-wide hem twice along the bottom edge of the skirt; topstitch.

4 Cut enough 2-inch-wide bias strips to cover the needed amount of piping cord to cover all sides of the slipcover top plus 6 inches for overlap. See steps 16–18 on *pages 24–25* for piping assembly instructions.

5 Use the bias strips to cover the piping cord. Sew the covered piping cord around the top. Place the cording-trimmed top on the ottoman, then pin the skirt to the top, forming an inverted pleat at each corner. Remove the skirt from the top, allowing the pins to hold the pleats in place. Press the pleats. With right sides facing, pin and then sew the skirt to the top.

6 Place the slipcover on the ottoman and wrap the belt around the sides. Buckle the belt tightly to hold the sides of the slipcover snug against the side of the ottoman. If one belt is too short, buckle two or more together to fit the circumference of the ottoman.

feel-good *Felt*

It's soft, it's fun, and it's easy to work with. Felt is an up-and-coming fabric that can brighten a daybed or any furniture piece that needs a fresh, funky look.

what you'll need

cream-color fabric
fabric tape measure; fabric scissors
felt in desired colors
thread; sewing needle
polyester fiberfill
aqua fabric
sewing machine with needle suited to the fabric
hook-and-loop tape

here's how

1 Cut cream-color fabric to fit over the ends of the daybed, leaving ⅝ inch extra fabric on each side.

2 Cut favorite shapes from various colors of felt, and zigzag-stitch them to the cream fabric.

3 Create fabric pom-poms by cutting a circle of felt and running a stitch around the perimeter ¼ inch from the edge. Tuck fiberfill in the circle; then tug on the thread, gathering the fabric into a ball shape. Knot the thread. Sew the pom-poms in place.

4 Piece together felt strips of various colors and widths for the front end pieces using a paper pattern of your bed's shape and allowing ⅝ inch extra fabric.

5 Cut a strip of aqua fabric using pinking shears or a wavy rotary cutter, and sandwich it between the striped fabric and cream-color fabric. Stitch everything together without turning; the selvage edge should be exposed to create a ruffle.

6 To create the daybed's bottom rail cover, cut strips of felt in various widths and long enough to wrap to the back of the rail. Attach them to the rail back with hook-and-loop tape.

Clever Cover-ups

slipcover Basics

You can change the look of your furniture on a whim with slipcovers that give you as many looks as the patterns found in a fabric store.

MAKING A MUSLIN PATTERN

We recommend making a muslin pattern before you attempt the actual slipcover so you can double-check fit before cutting into decorator fabric. Add 4 to 6 inches to each measurement to make it easy to pin the pieces together, then sketch the pieces needed on a cutting diagram to determine how many yards of muslin you'll need. (Muslin usually comes in 45-inch widths). Press the muslin with an iron, if necessary.

Use a fabric-marking pencil or pen and the measurements for each component to draw pattern pieces onto the muslin. Label each piece (front, back, skirt, etc.); then use a straightedge to mark the vertical center of each. Cut out pieces with fabric scissors or a rotary cutter and cutting mat. Place each muslin pattern piece on the corresponding part of the furniture, aligning the marked centers and smoothing toward the edges. Pin each piece loosely to the adjoining pieces until all pieces are pinned together (*photo 1*). **Note: There will be several inches of fabric outside the pinned lines.** Step back from the furniture to check the fit; then make any necessary adjustments.

When you're satisfied with the fit, mark the pinned lines on the muslin (*photo 2*). Remove the muslin from the furniture, remove the pins, and draw a second line ½ inch outside all of the marked lines for seam allowances. Cut out each muslin component along the outer lines.

TACKLING THE DECORATOR FABRIC

Lay out the decorator fabric right side up, press it with an iron, and arrange the muslin pattern pieces—marked side up—on the straight or lengthwise grain. If you want, center the fabric's large motifs on the back or seat piece. Pin the muslin and decorator fabric together (*photo 3*); then cut out (*photo 4*). Label each piece on the wrong side using a fabric pencil.

Align the raw edges of two adjacent pieces (say, the front and seat) with right sides together, and sew using a ½-inch seam allowance (*photo 5*). Continue until all pieces are stitched together.

Turn the cover inside out; then slip over the chair. Mark where the hem should fall at several places along the bottom edge; then remove the slipcover. Press with an iron along the marked hemline, and cut the fabric 2 inches beyond the pressed line. To hem, press under 1 inch twice, and sew in place. Trim the corner seams to reduce bulk, press the seams open, and then turn the slipcover right side out. Slip the cover over the chair.

EMBELLISHING YOUR SLIPCOVER

If you want a unique look, dress up the slipcover with trimmings. Some will affect how you cut the decorator fabric; others can be added once the slipcover is stitched together.

To add a tailored ruffle along one edge, as in *photo 6*, measure the distance the ruffle will span, multiply by 1½ or 2 for folds, and then add seam allowances. Cut a strip of decorator fabric as long as your determined measurement and twice as wide as the finished width, plus 1 inch (our finished strip is 1 inch wide). Press under long edges ½ inch, press the strip in half lengthwise to conceal raw edges, and topstitch along the open side. Position the ruffle strip along the desired edge of the slipcover, pinning one short, raw edge to a slipcover seam allowance. Situate your needle in the center of the strip width, pinching the fabric into ½-inch folds and stitching down the folds as you sew through all layers (*photo 7*). Pin the second raw edge to a slipcover seam allowance, and sew the raw edges into the seams when stitching the slipcover together.

Pleats are easy, too—they're simply folds of fabric. To add a 1-inch pleat to your slipcover, add 4 inches to the width of the fabric piece that will be pleated; then cut your decorator fabric. With a T-pin, mark the spot where you want the pleat. Measure 2 inches to the right of the T-pin, and create a crease in the fabric, folding that spot back to the T-pin and pinning in place. Repeat on the left side of the T-pin. Sew the pleated piece to adjacent slipcover pieces. Make a tidy tab, if you'd like, in the desired size and shape, press the raw edges under ¼ inch, center the tab over the pleat, and topstitch the perimeter. Pin a bundle of velour pansies to the tab for an extra flounce (*photo 8*).

To create a "drop waist" look on the back of a slipcover, as on *page 4*, cut and sew the back piece so it doesn't reach the floor. Measure and cut a skirt piece so it covers all four sides of the chair. Complete the top part of the slipcover first; then pin the skirt as shown in *photo 9*, and sew.

Clever Cover-ups 35

tailored Headboard

A padded headboard feels cozy in a bedroom. This print-covered beauty hides a plywood frame that is cut with gentle curves.

what you'll need

kraft paper and pencil
two ¾-inch-thick medium-density fiberboard (MDF)
    or plywood panels
circular saw and jigsaw
sandpaper
screws
1-inch-thick soft-grade foam
marking pen
spray adhesive
muslin
measuring tape
T-pins
upholstery fabric (we used approximately 7 yards)
fabric scissors
matching sewing thread
sewing machine with needle suited to fabric
welting (purchased or made)
staple gun and ⅝-inch staples
felt

here's how

Note: These instructions include making a muslin pattern to ensure proper fit before cutting the upholstery fabric. Sew with right sides facing and ½-inch seam allowances unless noted.

1 Decide on the size of your headboard; our headboard is wider than the mattress. Referring to the photograph, *opposite*, draw the headboard shape onto kraft paper and cut out. Trace around the paper template on each MDF or plywood panel with a pencil. Cut on the traced lines, using a circular saw for straight cuts and a jigsaw for curves. Sand the edges smooth. Screw the shapes together.

2 Place the template on the 1-inch-thick foam. Using a pencil or marking pen, draw a line about 2 inches beyond the edges of the template. Cut out the foam shape and attach it to the headboard base with spray adhesive. Roll the excess foam over the edges and secure it to the sides of the base with the adhesive. Trim the foam even with the back of the base.

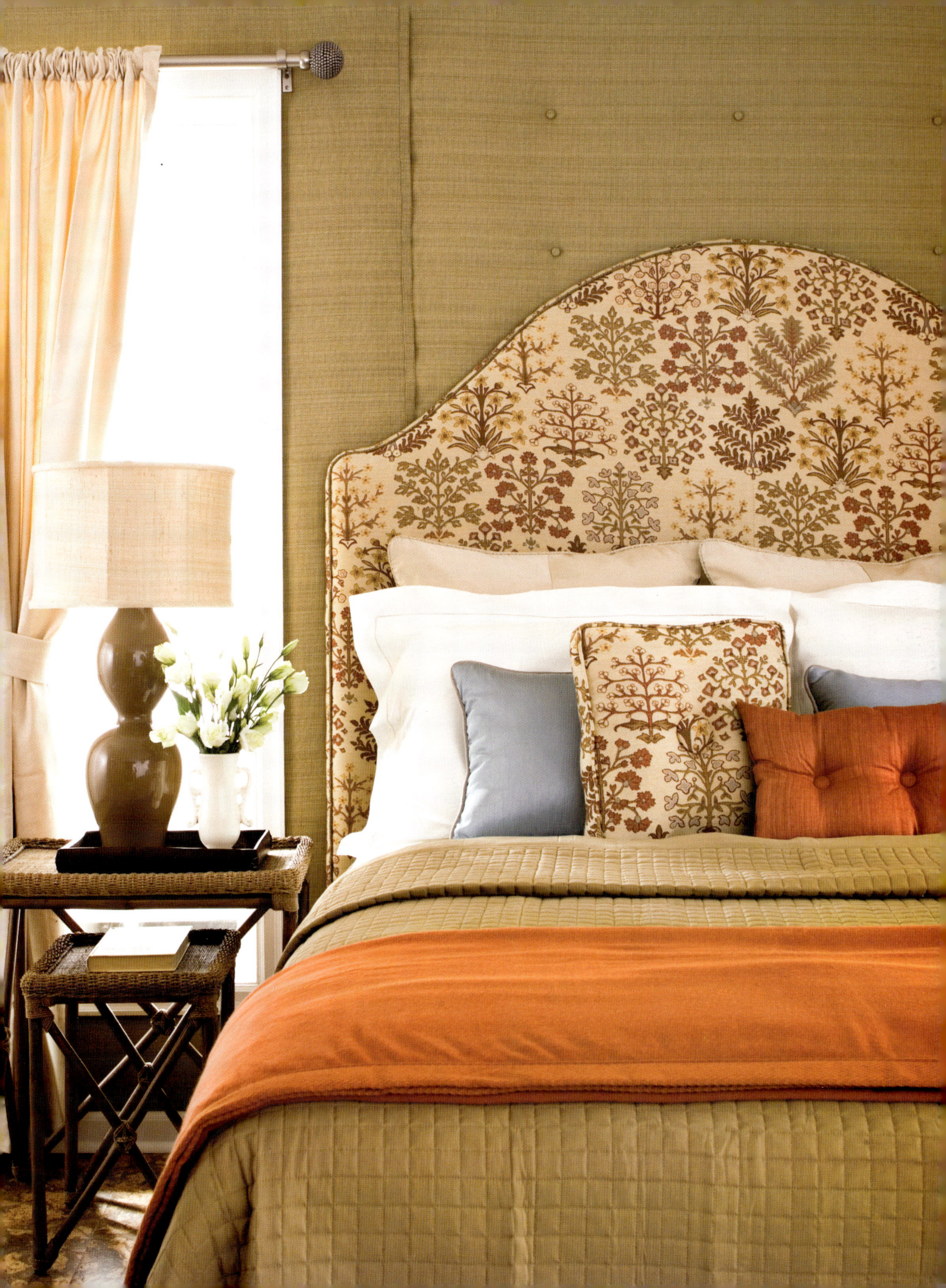

3 Draw two template shapes onto the muslin. Cut out 1 inch beyond the side and top edges to allow for seam allowances and ease. Cut out 3 inches beyond all the other drawn lines to allow for overlap along the bottom and inner legs. Cut enough 3½-inch-wide boxing strips from muslin to reach from one lower edge of the headboard to the opposite lower edge along the top line, plus 6 inches. Sew the short ends of the strips together to make a long strip. Press the seam allowances open.

4 Use T-pins to secure a muslin piece on the headboard front. Pin the boxing strip to the front muslin shape and then to the back one. Check the fit of the muslin cover on the foam-covered base, adjusting as necessary. When you are pleased with the fit, carefully remove the muslin cover. Use a pencil to mark the side and top cutting lines ½ inch outside the pinned lines to allow for seams on the front, back, and boxing strip. Cut along the marked lines as you remove pins.

5 Use the muslin pieces as patterns to cut a front and back from upholstery fabric, watching for the straight of the grain and for the placement of large motifs. Depending on the size of the headboard, it may be necessary to seam the fabric to achieve the needed width. Use the width and length of the muslin boxing strip to cut boxing strips from the upholstery fabric. Sew the short ends of the strips together to make one long strip. Press the seam allowances open.

6 Sew welting around the side and top edges of the front and back upholstery shapes. Pin the boxing strip to the front upholstery shape, sandwiching the welting between the fabric layers; sew the boxing strip to the front. Sew the opposite long edge of the boxing strip to the back upholstery shape in the same manner. Clip the corners and curved seams. Turn the cover right side out.

7 Slip the fabric cover over the foam-covered base. Beginning at the center bottom edge of the main headboard section and working outward toward the legs, pull the excess fabric from the back toward the front and staple in place on the underside of the base, positioning the staples close to the front of the headboard.

8 Trim the fabric that reaches beyond the staples. Pull the excess fabric from the front toward the back. Neatly fold under the raw edge of the fabric from the front and staple in place, covering the previous staples. Continue with the inner legs, trimming the fabric as needed and clipping carefully at the corners.

9 Wrap excess fabric around the bottoms of the legs and trim. Cut felt for the bottom of each leg; glue in place.

Deck the Walls

Upholstery can soften the walls in any room, keep it warmer, and muffle sound.

When covering a wall, choose an upholstery-weight fabric and plan ahead for a symmetrical layout of fabric panels. (Maximum width is usually 54 inches.) Here, the panels around the windows were made narrower so that the panel between them would be the same width as the one at the corner. Just how much fabric will you need? For a 12×8-foot wall, plan on at least 9 yards of upholstery fabric.

Use an electric staple gun to attach quilt batting to the wall and then stretch 54-inch-wide fabric panels over it, stapling at the edge of each panel. To tuft the wall panels, staple through the fabric and batting and then hide the staples by hot-gluing on fabric-covered buttons. Hide the seams between the panels by hot-gluing on trim or French seam tape.

printed Perfection

Pick out new upholstery fabric and stencil it with meaningful words or phrases to revitalize an armchair.

Clever Cover-ups 39

what you'll need

pliers
fabric scissors
upholstery fabric
letter or word stencils
acrylic paint
stencil brush
cloth
iron and ironing board
staple gun and staples
cord trim
hot-glue gun and glue sticks

here's how

1 Remove the old tacks fastening the fabric to the chair's framework. Save the old upholstery to use as templates for the new fabric. Remove the old foam from the chair's skeleton; save to use as a template.

2 Cut new foam to fit the chair's shape, using the old foam as a pattern. Using the old upholstery as a pattern, cut new fabric to cover the chair. Take note of the direction of each pattern piece so your lettering will be stenciled right side up.

3 Stencil each pattern piece with letters or words, rubbing the acrylic paint into the fabric with a stencil brush. Cover any fabric areas that you're not working on with a cloth to prevent spills or spattered paint from ruining your work. Let the paint dry. With a dry iron, press the wrong side of the fabric to heat-set the paint into the fabric.

4 Position the foam on the chair, and position the new fabric over the foam. Starting at the corners of the seat, secure the fabric to the underside of the chair's framework with a staple gun, pulling the fabric taut as you go and folding curves and corners as necessary. Finish the chair back in the same manner, securing the front first, and then the back, folding under the raw edges.

5 Use hot glue to attach a cord to the bottom edge of the seat.

pretty in *Piping*

You'll be proud to show off your upholsterying talents when you display a pretty slipper chair blanketed in your favorite color.

what you'll need

- camera
- armless chair
- pliers
- box cutter and seam ripper
- marking pen
- fabric scissors
- ½-inch-thick bonded polyester batting
- staple gun and staples, about ⅜ inch
- upholstery fabric (we used approximately 5 yards)
- tailor's chalk
- measuring tape
- upholstery-weight thread
- 5/32-inch welt cord or purchased welting
- upholstery tacks
- upholstery needles
- 1-inch-wide cardboard strip
- tack strips
- hammer and rubber bands
- kraft paper
- lightweight woven lining fabric
- black fine-woven fabric
- two 1-inch buttons to cover
- Perfect Glue #1 or other fabric glue
- sewing machine with needle suited to fabric
- thread

here's how

1 Photograph the chair before it is stripped of its original covering. Take overall and detail photos to use for reference when reupholstering.

2 Remove the original chair fabric, taking care not to tear any of the pieces, as they will be used for patterns. Use pliers to remove the staples, and use scissors, a box cutter, or a seam ripper to separate the pieces at the seams. Label the pieces noting the direction of the piece on the chair, the welting, and where pieces are sewn together. Save all the pieces to use as patterns or for measuring.

3 If needed, cut ½-inch-thick pieces of batting to cover the chair back and seat. Staple the additional layers of batting to the chair frame. Cover the chair back first, stapling it down. To prevent visible indents from the staples, pull gently on the batting around each staple so the staple is inside the batting. Staple batting to the seat.

4 Lay the original fabric pieces right sides up on the new fabric, watching for the straight of the grain, placement of any motifs, and pattern direction. Leave 2 to 3 inches of excess fabric beyond the stapled edges of the original pieces; this will allow for fabric to grasp when stapling (the original pieces were trimmed after they were stapled). Pin the pieces to the upholstery fabric and cut out the shapes 2 to 3 inches beyond the stapled edges of the original pieces and along all the other edges. Transfer the markings for direction, welting, and seams onto the new pieces with chalk.

5 Determine the length of welting needed and cut enough 1½- to 2-inch-wide bias strips to equal that length. Join the strips with diagonal seams and trim the seam allowance to ½ inch. Fold the bias strip around the cord and use a zipper foot to sew close to the cord.

6 Pin the fabric pieces together, right sides together, on the chair using the photos as a guide. If necessary, trim the excess fabric to make it fit snugly. Remove the pinned cover and sew the seams using the same seam allowances as the original upholstery pieces, with welting reinforcing the seams. Place the sewn cover back on the chair.

7 Cut welting for each side of the chair long enough to reach all the way from the front bottom corner of a back side piece to the back bottom corner. Sew a length of welting to the right and left side back pieces, beginning at the bottom front corner and stopping at the point where the outside back starts; the welting will be attached to the outside back later. Sew the side pieces to the inside back with the welting sandwiched between the fabric layers.

8 Place the assembled pieces on the chair back. Use upholstery tacks to temporarily tack the fabric in place; then staple at the back of the head rail, down the backs of the upright rails, and at the underside of the inside back rail. Staple the welting down the backs of the upright rails. Fold the pleats at the top of each side piece where needed to ease the fabric around the curves, and staple in the center. Glue on a covered button to hide the staples that hold the pleats in place.

9 Lay the new seat fabric on the chair seat. Pin the seat sides to the seat fabric, making any necessary adjustments to fit. Remove the fabric from the chair and sew the welting to the right side of the seat fabric, starting and ending at the back corners. Sew the seat sides to the seat fabric, clipping the corners. Slip the assembled seat cover onto the chair. Temporarily tack it in place and then staple it to the underside of the front, side, and back rails of the frame. Overlap the seat cover at the back sides with the left and right side back pieces. Use a circular needle to sew the overlapped edges in place, and staple the bottom edge of the right and left side back pieces to the underside of the side rails.

10 With right sides together, align the top edges of the outside back and the inside back, temporarily resting the outside back over the inside back of the chair. Put a few staples in about ½ inch from the top edges of the fabric to hold the fabric in place.

11 Cut a length of 1-inch-wide cardboard strip 2 inches less than the width of the chair back. Place the cardboard strip over the fabric edges; staple in place through the strip and the fabric.

12 Flip the fabric down over the back of the chair. Cut a length of tack strip for each side edge of the outside back. Fold the fabric at each side edge over a tack strip so the points are toward the chair back.

13 Tape the tack strips in place using a hammer covered with batting to protect the fabric. (Use rubber bands to hold the batting on the hammer.) The fabric should be tight against the welting. Pull the bottom edge of the fabric to the underside of the back rail and staple in place.

14 Use original skirt pieces for patterns or cut patterns from kraft paper to add a skirt. This skirt consists of upper and lower side pieces and a corner piece. The length of the skirt pieces is determined by your chair. The width of the upper side piece is 5 inches narrower than each side of the chair; the lower side pieces and the corner pieces are all 10 inches wider. Cut the paper patterns, and pin or tape them together to check for fit. Make adjustments as needed and add 1 inch to both the length and width measurements to allow for ½-inch seam allowances.

15 Cut four upper sides, eight lower sides, and four corners from upholstery and lining fabric. With right sides facing, sew the skirt and lining pieces together in pairs along the side and bottom edges. Clip the corners, turn right side out, and press. Baste together the top edges of each piece.

16 Overlap the skirt pieces to fit on the chair; pin the overlapped areas together. Sew the skirt pieces together along the top edge. Sew welting along the top edge of the skirt, beginning and ending at the center back.

17 Cut the welting cord so the ends butt together; fold under the fabric at one end of the welting to cover the opposite end. Hand-sew the folded edge in place.

18 To attach the skirt, lay the chair on its back and place the front skirt right side down on the chair. Staple along the underside of the skirt's upper edge through all layers. For added stability, staple through a cardboard strip. Repeat on all sides.

19 Trim excess upholstery fabric along the stapled edges on the underside of the chair. Use the original black bottom cloth as a pattern to cut a piece of black fabric. Cover the underside of the chair with the new black fabric by stapling it to the underside of the front, back, and side rails.

20 Cover the buttons with upholstery fabric. Using a strong fabric adhesive, glue a button to the back side of each chair at the center of the pleats.

the look of Leather

Because of its small scale, this cube-shape ottoman easily tucks under a sideboard or sofa table when not in use. Ours wears a tailored suit of imitation leather, but the rich cabernet color, pebbled texture, and nailhead trim leave visitors wondering whether it's the real thing.

what you'll need

- 14-inch cube made of ¾-inch plywood
- drill
- ½-inch drill bit
- jigsaw
- sandpaper
- primer
- paint, such as red brick
- spray adhesive
- 11-inch-square piece of upholstery foam
- 14-inch-square piece of muslin
- metal straightedge
- staple gun and ⅜-inch staples
- utility knife
- fabric glue
- 4—15-inch-square pieces of faux leather
- 16-inch-square piece of faux leather
- roll of nailhead trim
- fabric scissors
- 1⁄16-inch drill bit
- 4 furniture glides

here's how

1 Build a 14-inch bottomless cube from ¾-inch plywood. Drill a ½-inch-wide hole in the center of the cube top (this allows air to escape when weight is placed on the upholstered top). To create the legs, use a jigsaw to cut out a rectangle that is 3 inches from the corner and 2 inches up from the cube's bottom edge; repeat on the other three sides. Sand, wipe clean, prime, and paint the ottoman. Let dry.

2 Use spray adhesive to attach a square of upholstery foam to the center of the ottoman top. Lay the muslin square over the foam. Align a metal straightedge on one edge of the foam and the muslin square, and press firmly. Staple the muslin and foam to the plywood, using the straightedge as a guide. Pull the muslin tight and repeat on the opposite side. Repeat on the remaining two sides. Use a utility knife to trim the muslin.

3 Brush fabric glue on one side of the ottoman and one 15-inch square of faux leather. Center the fabric on the side of the cube; press and smooth out any trapped air. Let dry. Then use a utility knife to trim the edges of the fabric, including the notched base, flush with all other edges. Repeat on the remaining sides.

4 To cover the ottoman top, turn over the 16-inch-square piece of faux leather and mark a 2-inch-wide border around the square. Brush a coat of fabric glue on the border and around the foam cushion on the ottoman top. Allow the glue to dry. Position the fabric on top of the ottoman and use nailhead trim to attach it snugly to the cube on one edge. Pull the fabric tight and attach the opposite side with nailhead trim. Repeat on the remaining two sides. If necessary, brush on additional fabric glue between the fabric and the top border of the ottoman. Press the fabric firmly in place and let dry. Trim the excess fabric.

5 Attach a second border of nailhead trim around the cushion. If the nailhead trim does not line up exactly to allow a real nailhead to be on the end of a side, drill a 1⁄16-inch-wide hole into the last nailhead and attach the trim with an actual nail. Attach glides under each corner leg.

If you have basic sewing skills, you can master upholstery. Promise! To get started, choose a piece of furniture that offers simple lines.

upholstery *Basics*

1 Take photos of chair with the original fabric to use as a guide.

2 Strip off the original fabric carefully as the old pieces will be used as patterns. If needed, staple an additional layer of batting to the frame.

3 Use the old fabric pieces as patterns by laying them right side up on the right side of the new upholstery fabric.

4 Pin the new fabric pieces, wrong sides out, over the chair.

5 Use pleats to ease fabric around curves. Glue on a covered button to hide the center staple that holds the pleats in place.

6 To attach a back panel, stick tack strips through the wrong side of the fabric at both long edges, about 1 inch in.

7 Flip over the tack strips to pull the back panel taut and make clean, straight edges. Hammer the tacks into the frame with a hammer that has a piece of batting secured around the head.

8 Sew a sleeve of fabric for the chair seat and pull it on. Pull the back edge of the cover through the opening between the seat and back and staple it to the frame.

9 Pull the seat cover tight and tack it to the bottom of the chair frame on the front and sides.

10 Sew a lined, box-pleated skirt with welting. To assemble the skirt, arrange the layers on the chair, pin in place, and sew together at the top.

11 Staple the skirt to the frame on the wrong side of the fabric, just below the seam.

12 Use corner pleats to add delightful dressmaker details.

Clever Cover-ups 47

Better Homes and Gardens® Creative Collection™

Editorial Director John Riha

Editor in Chief Deborah Gore Ohrn

Executive Editor Karman Wittry Hotchkiss

Managing Editor Kathleen Armentrout

Contributing Editorial Manager Heidi Palkovic

Contributing Design Director Tracy DeVenney

Contributing Editor Susan Banker
Contributing Designer Wendy Musgrave
Contributing Project Designers Aimee Jackman, Angela Davidson, Jeni Hilpipre-Wright, Wanda J. Ventling
Contributing Photographers King Au, Kim Cornelison, D. Randolph Foulds, Bill Holt, Hopkins Associates, Pete Krumhardt, Greg Scheidemann
Copy Chief Mary Heaton
Contributing Copy Editor Mary Helen Schiltz
Proofreader Joleen Ross
Administrative Assistant Lori Eggers

Publishing Group President
Jack Griffin

Meredith CORPORATION

President and CEO Stephen M. Lacy

Chairman of the Board William T. Kerr

In Memoriam
E. T. Meredith III (1933–2003)

©Meredith Corporation, 2007.
All rights reserved. Printed in the U.S.A.
ISBN# 1-60140-595-2